"OUT OF THE MOUTHS OF SLAVES"

African American Oral History

I remember the soldiers calling to us saying, 'You are free!'

"Nine months I was trying to get away. I was secreted for a long time in a kitchen of a merchant..."

"There were nine of us... I stayed out of school a lot of days because I couldn't let my mother go to the cotton field alone and try to support all of us."

I could hardly believe what I heard—and it was my history, directly from my ancestors!

by
Carole Marsh

Black Jazz, Pizzazz & Razzmatazz ™

Editorial Assistant: Jenny Corsey • Graphic Design: Cecil Anderson

Copyright © 2003 Carole Marsh

Published by

GALLOPADE™
INTERNATIONAL

800-536-2GET
www.gallopade.com

Gallopade is proud to be a member of these educational organizations and associations:

The National School Supply and Equipment Association
The National Council for the Social Studies
Association for Supervision and Curriculum Development
Museum Store Association
Association of Partners for Public Lands

Black Jazz, Pizzazz, & Razzmatazz Books

Our Black Heritage Coloring Book

The Big Book of African American Activities

Black Heritage GameBook: Keep Score! Have Fun!
Find out how much you already know—and learn lots more!

Black Trivia: The African American Experience A-to-Z!

Celebrating Black Heritage:
20 Days of Activities, Reading, Recipes, Parties, Plays, and More!

Mini Timeline of Awesome African American Achievements and Events

"Let's Quilt Our African American Heritage & Stuff It Topographically!"

The Best Book of Black Biographies

The Color Purple & All That Jazz!: African American Achievements in the Arts

The Kitchen House: How Yesterday's Black Women Created Today's
Most Popular & Famous American Foods!

Black Business: African American Entrepreneurs & Their Amazing Success!

Other Carole Marsh Books

Meet Shirley Franklin: Mayor of Atlanta!

African American Readers—Many to choose from!

Table of Contents

"That on the 1st day of January, A.D. 1863, all persons held as slaves within any State or designated part of a State the people whereof shall then be in rebellion against the United States shall be then, thenceforward, and forever free; and the executive government of the United States, including the military and naval authority thereof, will recognize and maintain the freedom of such persons and will do no act or acts to repress such persons, or any of them, in any efforts they may make for their actual freedom.

—excerpt from _The Emancipation Proclamation_

A Word From the Author

Dear Readers,

The following book will tell you a very important story. The pages explain what life was like for the African slaves who came to live in America. You'll learn about important events and the lives of many people... fugitives, slaves, orators, abolitionists, slave owners, even children! After reading some of the stories, you may ask, "Did all this really happen?" The answer is yes. The experiences were real. The actions were real. And the lives were real.

History is written down so that people can learn about yesterday's mistakes and not make them again today. History makes folks think hard about their choices... what to say, what to think, what to do, and why all of this is important. History inspires lots of questions too. You will probably think of your own questions as you read this book. Here's a few to get you started on a thought process!

DISCUSSION QUESTIONS

- How did reading this book make you feel?
- Did you learn anything new by reading this book? What?
- What do you think the life of a slave child was like?
- How would you have felt about being a slave or a slaveholder?
- What is "oral history"? Does it communicate better than a textbook?
- Was there anything you read that you didn't understand? What?

Take advantage of this exciting wisdom! Take this chance to learn. Thank someone today for your own freedom!

Carole Marsh

FINAL THOUGHTS...

Sometime in the last few years, a relief organization sent out a call for bandages. They were collecting them to send to Rwanda, where so many black people had been killed and wounded in a terrible war. The organization received several large boxes from the United States. When they opened the boxes, they found long strips of clean white bandages carefully folded and packed. An enclosed note read: "We hope these help. We do not need them anymore." It was signed: The Ku Klux Klan.

JUST HOW DEEP ARE OUR ROOTS?

Alex Haley

"We were in Savannah, Georgia, getting ready to film a scene where Kunta Kinte refused to call himself by the name his master had given him. The master had decided Kunta's name would be "Toby." The overseer was given the word, and he passed it to the old slave who was training the young Kunta.

The old slave was being played by **Lou Gossett,** and the young slave, of course, by **Levar Burton**. But no matter what the old slave did, the young one refused to accept another name. Finally, word of his defiance went back via the overseer to the master, who ordered Kunta beaten until he would say his new name was now "Toby."

That was the scene to be filmed that day. Levar was brought out and tied with his wrists to a set of crossed poles, much like an Indian tepee. As he hung there, to his right sat the old slave, Lou Gossett. He was being punished for his inability to get the young slave to say the name and would be needed to help remove the young slave after what would surely be a terrible beating.

When the director announced "Action!" the overseer came out, dressed in a kind of cloak, proud and furious. He looked at the young one, hanging up there by his wrists, and he said, "What's your name, boy?"

Levar answered quietly, "Kunta."

Smirking, the overseer looked over at a tall, anonymous slave in the background who was holding a whip, and this slave walked out into camera range, raised his arm and began.

The whip they were using was made with loosely woven hemp, nothing that would hurt anybody. But a trained actor knows how to jerk the instant it touches his skin, making the force and sting of the blow appear painfully real. Levar took two blows, then a third, which, with the special effects blood capsules breaking, was almost too much to watch.

Then, again, the overseer asked, "What your name, boy?" Again, now weakly, Levar said, "Kunta."

After three more blows, and more blood, the 35 or so of us just out of camera range were so angry we were ready to charge out there and choke somebody.

This time Levar, his head nodding to one side, with no strength left even to lift his chin, said, in a whisper, "Toby, master." And the overseer whirled about, proud, arrogant. "*Louder!* Let me hear it again. *What's your name, boy?*"

Barely, Levar whispered, "Toby, master."

Then the tall slave who had done the beating cut Levar down, and Levar slumped into Lou Gossett's lap.

Gossett, an experienced veteran actor, was supposed to embrace the young slave, to comfort him. One camera was to slowly slide out of focus, as an optional way to end that two-hour episode.

But what happened is something that people who spend their lives around films being made may witness but a few times—when experienced actors or actresses totally forget who they are and become the role they are portraying, letting what's inside them take over.

When Levar slumped into Lou Gossett's lap, Lou's own body began convulsing. He curled into a near-fetal position, grasping Levar to his own shaking self—and out of Lou's voice box, through his tears, came a hoarse, guttural cry.

"What *difference* it make what they calls you? You knows who you is, you's Kunta!" He convulsed again. He let out another, even higher-pitched cry: "Dey's gonna be a better day."

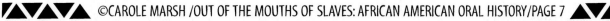

He paused. Silence. Then he repeated it.

"Dey's gonna be a better day!"

Maybe ten seconds passed, then the last film was clicked through three cameras. The only sound was Lou's weeping.

Then he pulled himself back out of the role, into the present.

"I don't know what happened to me," he said. "I forgot about who I am. I was there, a hundred and fifty years ago, and that was my little Guinea boy. I was supposed to teach him how to be a slave and instead he had taught me how to be a man." —as told by *Roots* author, Alex Haley.

*When your purpose is noble—
when your goals benefit mankind—
all that you need to achieve them will be available to you.*

WHAT WAS SLAVERY REALLY LIKE?

John Brickell was an Irish doctor who visited America in 1730. He published A *Natural History of North Carolina* in 1737. In that book, he described how important slaves were to planters, how "Negroes" were too valuable to be bought with mere paper money, how it took gold or silver to buy a "Black." He also outlined the differences between slaves brought directly from Africa and those born in America. The latter, he said, were raised as Christians and seemed better behaved, more obedient. The Africans, on the other hand, were defiant.

"I have frequently seen them whipt to that degree that large pieces of their Skin have been hanging down their Backs, yet I never observed one of them to shed a Tear."

THE SLAVES OF SOMERSET

One of the first children's mystery books I ever wrote was set on location at the historic house known as Somerset Place, near Creswell, North Carolina. The area is known as "the haunt of beasts."

This was one of the first children's fictional books to feature both black and white children as characters. I had selected some school children to portray the characters in the book: two from my family (they always got stuck being in my books until they got too big!), and two from the Creswell area.

It is one thing to read about slavery in your history books... and another to actually visit a plantation site where you can still see the buildings and the lands where the slaves lived and worked.

The nice thing about exploring history with young people is that they have open minds. Their questions were endless about how the slaves lived, why there was slavery, about the life of the master and his family, about the fascinating African traditions the slaves brought with them, about the food, the kids, and everything else.

So, here are just a few things about Somerset—a real slave plantation. It still exists. You can go and see it. In fact, it was one of the few plantations where a record of the names of the slaves was even kept. Recently the descendants of these original slaves gathered to ponder their past.

What were the slaves' names? Jack Bissell, Charles, Tom Evans, Edmund, Peter, Soloman, Jane, Ben, Pleasant, Daphne, Ned, Jack, Peter Blount, Mingo, Fortune, Bob, Dick, Cato, Amarillis, Charlotte, Joe, Dillale, and Teresa.

Somerset master **Josiah Collins** bought 32 slaves for $6,000—less than $200 a person. Some of these were (as recorded in the official record):

A negro woman named Celia aged about thirty six years together with her five children: negro Fanny aged about thirteen years, negro girl Kate aged about eight years, negro girl Peggy aged about six years, negro Milly aged about two years, and negro boy Isaac aged about three months; negro woman named Sylvia aged about thirty four years, together with her six children: negro boy Nelson aged about fourteen, negro boy Tom aged about twelve years, negro girl Carolina aged about eight years, negro girl Ann aged about six years, negro boy Granville aged about three years and negro boy Hamilton aged about two; negro woman named Elsy aged about thirty years, together with her six children: negro girl Amy aged about ten years, negro boy Fred aged about eight years, negro girl Mary aged about seven, negro boy Peter aged about five years, negro boy Jacob aged about two years and negro boy John aged about two months; mulatto woman named Teany aged about thirty years together with her four children: negro girl Penny aged about twelve years, negro girl Priscilla aged about nine years, negro boy John aged about seven years and negro boy Daniel aged about four years; negro woman named Patricia aged about thirty four years together with her two children: negro girl Eliza, aged about eleven years, and negro girl Catharine aged about ten years; negro woman named Sal aged about twenty four years, together with her two children: mulatto girl Carolina aged about eight years and negro Heather aged about one year; and negro girl Lavinia aged about fifteen years.

There were also African-sounding names on the list: Quaminy, Cuff, Tass, Cag, Eggy, Abijac; Spanish names like Serena and Patrina; a French name, Bridgette; and names from the Bible, such as Jericho, Hannah, David, Adam, and Soloman.

"extremely black, with elegant white teeth," and spoke "a most curious lingo..."

Many of Collins' slaves dug canals on the plantation so that the land could be drained. It took two awful years. Cages were built around the slaves who shoved the dirt through the bars. They had no protection from the sun, rain, or mosquitoes, which often carried malaria.

Many of the slaves died from illness or exhaustion. Slaves who were not able to leave the work site at the end of a day "would be left by the bank of the canal, and the next morning the returning gang would find them dead." The canals proved deadly for others too. Two of Collins' sons drowned in the canals along with two slave boys. But the plantation way of life did not go on forever.

The shadow of civil war spread across Somerset and the South. In 1865, Mary Collins returned to Somerset. Even though most of the slaves came back, they refused to work without pay or for the small shares of crops offered them. Most of them soon left the plantation.

Where did these slaves come from? A cargo of Africans was delivered to Edenton after the Revolution. During June of 1786, a visitor was in town when the brig Guineaman arrived from Africa with a hundred Negroes in her hold. All were between 20 and 25 years of age, "extremely black, with elegant white teeth," and spoke "a most curious lingo... ."

COMING TO AMERICA

The trip to America was a horrid experience. The typical slave ship was "tight packed" or crammed with as many bodies as it could carry. Slave traders usually lost about a third of their slaves during the voyage to heat, disease, and often suicide. Most of the slaves did not have clothing and had to sleep in their own excrement, and had no way to communicate with their captors since they did not speak their language.

DAY-TO-DAY LIFE

The master's diary gives us a glimpse of the troublesome, dull, chore-laden day-to-day life:

April 19 — Nine pounds to Nathaniel Allen "for 3 days hire of Caesar."

May 22 — Three pounds "paid Caleb Benbridge for apprehending Negro Sam."

May 24 — One shilling to Josiah Collins "for Beef & Bread for Negroes."

May 26 — Two pounds, nine shillings to Samuel Dickinson "for sundry medicines for Negroes this month."

May 26 — Six shillings to Ebenezer Spruill "for bringing home a runaway Negro."

June 11 — Four pounds, six shillings "paid Wilkins for apprehending Negro Sam."

June 27 — Eight shillings "for 4 qts. Rum for Negroes."

July 1 — Four pounds "paid Joseph Oliver for building two Negro houses."

July 10 — Twenty pounds, fourteen shillings "for 138 yds. Asnaburg for Negroes' clothes."

July 10 — Two pounds "pd. James Ambrose for taking up two Negroes."

August 21 — Seventeen pounds, fifteen shillings "paid for making 60 shirts, 43 shifts, 60 pr. trousers & 33 coats."

December 4 — Two pounds, sixteen shillings "paid John Alexander for hogs stolen by our Negroes."

December 4 — Four pounds "paid John Porter for taking up Smart and Sambo."

The slaves lived in barracks-like buildings. Often several families lived in a room. All slaves weren't "equal." Only the "house" servants could go in the plantation house. The field hands worked far from the mansion and were given the dirtiest jobs. Slaves who were skilled at a craft were sometimes even paid for their work. And the cooks were invaluable members of the household staff. There was even one free black at Somerset, a nursemaid, but her life was very lonely since she was not really part of the slave world or the white world.

Except for a one-day vacation at Thanksgiving and a week at Christmas, the slaves worked each weekday from sunup to sundown and Saturdays from sunup until noon.

Life was very dangerous. Once, a 20-year-old slave named Becky "lost both legs by amputation," after they were crushed by a falling log.

And there was always plenty of hard work for the men, women and children:

January – shuck corn

February – shuck corn

March – plow the fields; pull old cornstalks

April – planting time

May – pull weeds; clear ditches and canals

June – harvest wheat

July – harvest and store wheat

August – repair equipment

September – cut straw and hay and haul it

October – harvest corn; replow

November – load corn on flat boats and float to barn

December – clean, cut firewood, kill hogs

In addition, it took 25 house servants to cook the meals, tend the gardens, clean house, keep the eight fireplaces blazing, take care of the children, keep the carriage ready to go and much, much more.

On their own time, the slaves could grow extra crops, fish, or hunt bear, coons, possums, squirrels, geese, ducks, turkeys and quail. They could also raise hogs and chickens. Slaves who followed the rules earned credit that could be exchanged for goods such as food, clothing, skins, mirrors, knives, even fiddles at the plantation store.

When freedom finally came, the Somerset slaves, who were so very dependent on the plantation, did not even know what to do about it.

The slaves did manage to keep one of their African customs called "John Koonering." This was performed on Christmas Day. A slave dressed up in a costume of rags, and carried a small tin cup or bowl.

Other slaves dressed in ribbons, rags and feathers play musical instruments called "gumba boxes." They were followed by the rest of the slaves who came to the front door of the "Great House" and danced and played for the master. He was then expected to provide something in the tin cup as a reward.

Sounds a little like "trick or treat" to me. How about you?

One slave, Uriah Bennett said: "For months and months at a time we weren't allowed off the farm. Sometimes we would get as far as the gate and peep over. We were told that if we got outside the Padirollers would get us."

 ORAL # HISTORY

Interviews were conducted with slaves.

"I haven't anything to say against slavery," said **Samuel Riddick**. "My old folks put my clothes on me... they gave me shoes and stockings and put them on me when I was a little boy. I loved them, and I can't go against them in anything. There were things I did not like about slavery on some plantations, whuppin' and sellin' parents and children from each other, but I haven't much to say. I was treated good."

Blount Baker said of the Union troops: "We ain't seed no Yankees 'cept a few huntin Rebs. Dey talks mean ter us an' one of dem says dat we niggers am de cause of de war. 'Sir,' I says, 'folks what am a wantin' a war can always find a cause.' He kicks me in de seat of de pants fer dat, so I hushes."

A slave named **Mary Anderson** recalled the day the Yankees arrived: "Nobody was working, and slaves were walking over the grove in every direction. At nine o'clock all the slaves gathered at the great house, and marster and missus came out on the porch and stood side by side. You could hear a pin drop everything was so quiet. Then marster said, 'Good morning,' and missus said, 'Good morning, children.' They were both crying. Then marster said, 'Men, women, and children, you are free. You are no longer my slaves. The Yankees will soon be here.'

Marster and missus then went into the house, got two large armchairs, put them on the porch facing the avenue and sat down side by side and remained there watching. In about an hour, they saw a black cloud coming up the avenue from the main road. It was the Yankee soldiers! They finally filled the mile-long avenue reaching from the marster's house to the main road and spread out over the mile square grove. The mounted men dismounted. The footmen stacked their shining guns and began to build fires and cook. They called the slaves saying, 'You are free.' Slaves were whooping and laughing and acting like they were crazy. Yankee soldiers were shaking hands with the Negroes, calling them by name (Sam, Dinah, Sarah), and asking them questions. They busted the door to the smoke house and got all the hams. They went to the ice house, got several barrels of brandy, and had such a good time. The Negroes and Yankees were cooking and eating together. The Yankees told them to come on and join them because they were free. Marster and missus sat on the porch, and they were so humble no Yankee bothered anything in the Great House.

"... They called the slaves saying, 'You are free.' Slaves were whooping and laughing..."

The slaves were awfully excited. The Yankees stayed there, cooked, ate, drank and played music until about night, then a bugle began to blow and you never saw such gettin' on horses and lining up in your life. In a few minutes they began to march, leaving the grove which was soon as silent as a grave yard. When they left the country, a lot of the slaves went with them and soon there were none of marster's slaves left. They wandered around for a year from place to place, fed and working most of the time at some other slave owner's plantation and getting more homesick every day.

The second year after the surrender our marster and missus got on their carriages and went and looked up all the Negroes they heard of who ever belonged to them. Some who went off with the Yankees were never heard of again. When marster and missus found any of theirs they would say, 'Well, come on back home.' When they got back marster would say, 'Well, you have come back home have you?' And the Negroes would say, 'Yes, marster.' Most all spoke of them as missus and marster as they did before the surrender, and getting back home was the greatest pleasure of all."

FOLLOWIN' THE FINGER

"Followin' the finger" is how one slave described her life. "They point and you follow and do." Such was the life on a South Carolina lowcountry plantation called Tombee. Like Somerset, this plantation was one of the few where the master kept detailed records. In fact, **Thomas Chaplin** kept a journal that spanned almost 30 years. Chaplin was born wealthy, but he lost everything. Even when he owned Tombee, Chaplin was rich in land and slaves, but he seldom had even $10 in his own pocket to spend.

> "Cuffee" was a common Negro name, from the Fanti (a West African language), given to a boy born on a Friday.

TIMELINE OF AFRICAN AMERICAN HISTORY

1829

A free black, **David Walker**, publishes an essay which encourages slaves to revolt. As a result, most southern states make it illegal to teach slaves to read and write.

1830

Anti-Slavery Movement
Black people fight slavery by lecturing for abolitionist societies, writing and publishing newspapers, and organizing channels of escape through the Underground Railroad.

1831

Maria Stewart is the first black woman to lecture against slavery.

William Lloyd Garrison publishes the first edition of the newspaper, *Liberator*, which called for emancipation of slaves.

Nat Turner leads a slave rebellion in Southampton, Virginia.

1833

The **American and the Female Anti-Slavery Societies** are formed in Philadelphia with a convention.

1833

Oberlin College is the first coed college founded to educate African Americans.

1837

The first **Anti-Slavery Convention of American Women** is held in New York.

1839

Joseph Cinque leads a successful revolt on the slave ship, *Amistad.*

1850

Congress passes the **Fugitive Slave Act** requiring captured runaway slaves to be returned to their owners. Whites now hunt slaves for profit.

1853

Sarah Parker Remond, (1826-1887), is refused a seat in the Howard Athenaeum in New York. She takes the case to the police court, and the defendants are fined. In 1859 and 1860, she lectures against American slavery in Great Britain.

1854

Frances Ellen Watkins Harper, (1825-1911), delivers her first anti-slavery lecture and publishes her first book of verse. She becomes widely respected because of her dedication to her people, her eloquent speaking, and her writing ability for the abolitionist cause.

1857

With the **Dred Scott Decision**, the U.S. Supreme Court denies citizenship to black people.

1859

Planning a black insurrection, white abolitionist, **John Brown**, leads a raid at Harper's Ferry. He is captured and sentenced to death.

1861

Civil War

"And then we saw the lightning, and that was the guns; and then we heard the thunder, and that was the big guns; and then we heard the rain falling, and that was the drops of blood falling; and when we came to get in the crops, it was dead men that we reaped." — *a slave*

1861

Charlotte Forten Grimke, (1837-1914), becomes a volunteer teacher of freed men on St. Helena Island in South Carolina. Her writings later become a valuable documentation of the black struggle for freedom during the Civil War.

1863

Harriet Tubman, (1820-1913), leads a military raid on the Combahee River in South Carolina and helps hundreds of slaves escape to freedom.

1865

The **Thirteenth Amendment** abolishes slavery.

The **Freedmen's Bureau** is established by Congress and funded by a cotton tax to provide schools, relief, and legal aid to freed slaves. It was abolished in 1872.

1877

The **Hayes Compromise** ends Reconstruction by withdrawing federal troops from the South.

1880

Post Reconstruction
The policy of white supremacy in the South leaves black people segregated, disenfranchised (without opportunity), and oppressed. The struggle for freedom is carried on by black churches, newspapers, schools, and national organizations which devote themselves to solidarity and self-help.

1895

First National Conference of Colored Women is held in Boston; marks the beginning of a black women's club movement.

1896

The U.S. Supreme Court upholds segregation in its "separate but equal" doctrine set forth in the **Plessy vs. Ferguson** case.

Mary Church Terrell, (1863-1954), graduates from the Women's Medical College of Pennsylvania. She will become the first woman to practice medicine in South Carolina, where she eventually will found two hospitals and three clinics.

1909

The **NAACP** is founded. It crusades against lynching and segregation, and attempts to secure rights for black people.

1920

The **Nineteenth Amendment** gives women the right to vote.

1940

Ella Jo Baker, (1903-1987), a dedicated organizer in the freedom movement, begins work in the South as field secretary of the NAACP.

1941

Civil Rights Movement

Thousands of black people organize to press their demands for justice. This social movement is committed to nonviolent resistance. As a result of the threatened march on Washington, D.C., organized by A. Philip Randolph, President Roosevelt issues an executive order against discrimination of workers in defense industries and government.

1942

Margaret Walker, (b. 1915), wins the Yale Award for Young Poets for her moving collection of poems, ***For My People***.

1947

Lawyer and economist, **Sadie T.M. Alexander**, (1898-1989), is appointed to Truman's Commission on Civil Rights which prepares the report ***To Secure These Rights***, attacking racial injustice in the U.S.

CORE sends its first group of "Freedom Riders" through the South.

1948

In response to actions taken by the **League for Nonviolent Civil Disobedience Against Military Segregation**, headed by **A. Philip Randolph**, President Truman issues an executive order banning segregation in the armed forces.

Pharmacist **Ella Nora Phillips Stewart**, (1893-1987), is elected president of the National Association of Colored Women. She will later write *Lifting As They Climb*, a history of this organization.

Edith Irby Jones, (b. 1927), is the first black to be admitted to a Southern medical school, The University of Arkansas.

1954

In the ***Brown vs. Board of Education Case***, the U.S. Supreme Court declares segregation in public schools unconstitutional.

1955

The **U.S. Supreme Court** orders school integration "with all deliberate speed."

In Montgomery, Alabama, **Rosa Parks**, (b. 1913), refuses to give up her seat on a public bus to a white man. She is arrested and jailed. The Montgomery Improvement Association is organized, Rev. Martin Luther King, Jr., is elected president, and a year-long bus boycott results in the U.S. Supreme Court invalidating segregation on Montgomery buses.

1957

As president of the state NAACP, **Daisy Gatson Bates**, (b. 1922), leads the fight for school integration in Little Rock, Arkansas.

1960

First student sit-ins at a lunch counter in Greensboro, North Carolina.

1961

More than **50,000 people demonstrate for equal rights** in 100 cities, and over 3,600 are jailed.

1963

Dr. Martin Luther King, Jr., delivers his "I Have a Dream" speech during the March on Washington for jobs and freedom, attended by 250,000 people. The march is the largest human rights demonstration in U.S. History.

Gloria Richardson, (b. 1922), is the only black woman to lead a local civil rights group. She heads the Cambridge Nonviolent Action Committee in Maryland.

Charlayne Hunter-Gault, (b. 1942), is the first black woman to receive a degree (B.A. in journalism) from the University of Georgia.

1964

Fannie Lou Hamer, (1917-1977), is a founder and vice chairperson of the Mississippi Freedom Democratic Party. A popular speaker, Hamer becomes a symbol of black determination to overcome discrimination.

1964

The **Civil Rights Act** prohibits discrimination in public facilities; in employment on the basis of sex, religion, nationality; and establishes the Equal Employment Opportunity Commission.

Lawyer, **Marion Wright Edelman**, (b. 1939), establishes the NAACP's Legal Defense and Education Fund Office in Jackson, Mississippi.

1965

Septima Poinsette Clark, (1898-1987), leads an Southern Christian Leadership Conference (SCLC) group which registers about 7,000 black voters in Alabama.

Voting Rights Act allows blacks to vote freely and unhindered.

1966

Rubye Doris Smith Robinson, (1942-1967), becomes the executive secretary of SNCC and strongly supports black nationalism.

Black Panther Party forms to establish black power in America.

1967

Dr. Martin Luther King, Jr., is assassinated in Memphis, Tennessee. He delivered his last speech, "I Have Been to the Mountaintop," the day prior.

President Lyndon B. Johnson appoints the first black U.S. Supreme Court Justice, **Thurgood Marshall**.

1968

New York elects **Shirley Chisholm** as first African American U.S. Congresswoman.

1969

Mary Moultrie, (b. 1942), leads a wage strike at the Medical College Hospital in South Carolina.

1972

Political activist and intellectual, **Angela Davis**, (b. 1944), is acquitted of murder in a political trial in California.

Equal Employment Opportunity Act passes.

1974

The **Coalition of Labor Union Women** is formed.

1978

U.S. Postal Service issues a **Black Heritage** postage stamp series.

1983

Martin Luther King, Jr. Day is first celebrated on January 20th as a federal holiday.

1989

General Colin Powell chosen as first black chairman of Joint Chiefs of Staff, the nation's top military position. He is later appointed by President George W. Bush as U.S. Secretary of State.

1991

Civil Rights Act limits affirmative action.

1992

Mae Jemison becomes the first African American female U.S. astronaut.

1993

Toni Morrison becomes first African American female to win a Pulitzer Prize in literature for her novel, *Beloved*.

2000

President George W. Bush appoints African American **Condoleezza Rice** to serve as his U.S. National Security Advisor.

2002

Tiger Woods becomes the youngest golfer (age 26!) to win 8 PGA major titles. African American tennis star **Serena Williams** wins the U.S. Open and Wimbledon tournaments.

Talk show host **Oprah Winfery** receives the first Bob Hope Humanitarian Award at the 54th Annual Emmy Awards

"Manumission" occurred when an owner decided to free a slave. Possible reasons could include a slave's old age or illness, or gratitude for exemplary service. Also, some owners became Christians and no longer believed in slavery.

"QUOTATIONS"

"Slavery is the negro system of labor."
—William J. Grayson, author, *The Hireling and the Slave*

"Last of the holidays & I am glad for then the Negroes will go to work & there will be something for me to do."
—*Thomas B. Chaplin's Plantation Journal*

October 6, 1827 advertisement in the Tarborough Free Press:

$50 REWARD: Ranaway from the Subscriber, living in the county of Edgecombe, NC about eight miles north of Tarborough, on the 24th of August last, a negro fellow named Washington, about 24 years of age, 5 feet and 8 or 10 inches high, dark complexion, stout built, and an excellent field hand, no particular marks about him recollected.

HOW COME?

When I was born I was black.
When I grew up I was black.
When I'm sick I'm black.
When I go out into the sun I'm black.
When I die I'll be black
But you:
When you were born you were pink.
When you grow up you are white.
When you get sick you are green.
When you go out in the sun you are red.
When you go out in the cold you are blue.
When you die you turn purple.
And you call me colored?

Runaways held in the New Bern jail in 1767:

Two New Negro Men, the one named Joe, about 45 years of age... much wrinkled in the face, and speaks bad English. The other is a young fellow... speaks better English than Joe, whom he says is his father, has a large scar on the fleshy part of his left arm. ...They have nothing with them but an old Negro cloth jacket, and an old blue sailor's jacket without sleeves. Also... a Negro named Jack, about 23 years of age,... of a thin visage, blear-eyed,... has six rings of his country marks around his neck, his ears are full of holes.

SLAVE NARRATIVES

George Moses Horton, a Chatham County slave, wrote poetry for sale to Chapel Hill students, who saw no irony in paying a black man to do their literary wooing for them. For himself he wrote:

"How long have I in bondage lain,
And languished to be free!
Alas! and I still complain —
Deprived of liberty.
When Israel was in Egypt's land,
O let my people go!
Oppressed so hard they could not stand,
O let my people go!
CHORUS — O go down Moses
Away down to Egypt's land,
And tell King Pharaoh
To let my people go!"

"The whole area before the pulpit, and in the distant aisles of the forest, became one vast, surging sea of sound, as negroes and whites, slaves and free-men, saints and sinners, slave-holders, slave-hunters, slave-traders, ministers, elders, and laymen alike joined in the pulses of that mighty song. A flood of electrical excitement seemed to rise with it, as, with a voice of many waters, the rude chant went on."

—from *A Tale of the Great Dismal Swamp*

"I was born on a plantation near Fayetteville, North Carolina, and I belonged to J.B. Smith. He owned about 30 slaves. When a slave was no good, he was put on the auction block in Fayetteville and sold. The slave block stood in the center of the street, Fayetteville Street, where Ramsey and Gillespie Street came in." —*Sarah Louise Augustus*

A former slave, **John H. Jackson**, remembered the building of Thalian Hall: "I was born in 1851, in the yard where my owner lived next door to the City Hall. I remember when they was finishin' up the City Hall. I also remember the foreman, Mr. James Walker, he was general manager. The overseer was Mr. Keen. I remember all the bricklayers; they all was colored. The man that plastered the City Hall was named George Price, he plastered it inside. The men that plastered the City Hall outside and put those columns up in the front, their names was Robert Finey and William Finey, they both was colored. Jim Artis now was a contractor an' builder. He done a lot of work 'round Wilmington. Yes'm, they was slaves, mos' all the fine work 'round Wilmington was done by slaves. They called 'em artisans. None of 'em could read, but give 'em any plan an' they could foller it to the las' line."

"Tenants ain't got no chance. I don't know who gets the money, but it ain't the poor. It gets worse every year—the land gets more wore out, the prices for tobacco gets lower, and everything you got to buy gets higher. Like I told you, I'm trying to 'be content' like the Bible says and not to worry, but I don't see no hope." - from *Mothers of the South*

An early victim of slave trading was **Gustavus Vassa**. He was born in Benin, in what is now Nigeria, in 1745. At age 11, he was kidnapped from his family and sold into slavery. Later he was sold again to traders and chained on a slave ship bound for America. He was sold to a Virginia planter, and then to a British naval officer, and finally to a Philadelphia merchant who gave him the chance to buy his freedom. As a ship's steward, he traveled widely. He also worked to bring an end to the slave trade. In 1791, Vassa wrote his autobiography. It contains a passage describing the voyage of the slave ship that carried him to America.

Antislavery newspapers began in 1821, when the white editor **Benjamin Lundy** launched his *Genius of Universal Emancipation* with six subscribers. It was even harder to start the first black newspaper, *Freedom's Journal*. It was founded in New York in March 1827 by **John B. Russwurm** and **Samuel E. Cornish**. Young Russwurm had just graduated from Bowdoin with the first college degree given a black in the United States. When he sailed for Liberia in 1829 to become the new republic's superintendent of education, the Reverend Cornish carried on as editor.

David Walker didn't have to be told that if a slave struck his master it meant death. Freeborn in North Carolina, but the son of a slave father, he knew slavery—what the South called the "peculiar institution"—firsthand. His hatred of slavery drove him to Boston, where he sold old clothes and subscriptions to the "Freedom's Journal." He burned to deliver his own message to the slaves, and in 1829 he published his pamphlet, Walker's Appeal.

In 1831, a year after **David Walker** vanished, slave **Nat Turner**, led 70 blacks in a revolt that slaughtered 57 men, women, and children in rural Southampton County, Virginia. Troops rushed in to put down the uprising and killed over one hundred blacks—the innocent as well as the insurrectionists—in a savage massacre. Wild rumors and alarms swept through the South. The threat of slave revolt made sleep uneasy.

But it was not the first time. Rebellions began in the 1600s, aboard the first slave ships bound for the American colonies. As slaves continued to fight for their freedom, the bondage laws were made harsher and harsher. **Gabriel Prosser's** large-scale plot to attack Richmond with a thousand men in 1800 was betrayed at the last moment and the slave preacher and his followers hanged. Another plot that involved 9,000 blacks led by the free black **Denmark Vesey**, was exposed in Charleston in 1822. Vesey and 36 others were executed.

The purpose of slavery was to provide the labor that could bring profits to the master. Most Southern farmers had small holdings and few or no slaves. The wealthy slaveholders, who ruled Southern economy and politics, owned huge plantations with hundreds or thousands of slaves. Despite the estate size, an efficient owner made money with his slaves. Up until the Civil War it was more profitable for the planter to keep his workers in bondage than to use free labor.

Defenders of slavery claimed the bondsmen cheerfully accepted their condition. But how did the slave look at the year-round routine of growing cotton? Ex-slave **Solomon Northup** left behind his own record of what life was like in Louisiana. Northup, born free in New York, was kidnapped in Washington during 1841, and enslaved for 12 years on a cotton plantation near the Red River in Louisiana. A Northerner later wrote Northup's story in 1853, the same year he was freed. *Twelve Years a Slave*, from which a slave escape is vividly detailed, sold 27,000 copies in just two years.

"...NINE MONTHS I was trying to get away. I was secreted for a long time in a kitchen of a merchant near the corner of Franklyn and 7th streets, at Richmond, where I was well taken care of, by a lady friend of my mother. When I got tired of staying in that place, I wrote myself a pass to pass myself to Petersburg. Here I stopped with a very prominent colored person, who was a friend to freedom. I stayed here until two white friends told other friends if I was in the city to tell me to go at once, and stand not upon the order of going, because they had heard a plot.

I wrote a pass, started for Richmond, reached Manchester, got off the cars, walked into Richmond, once more got back into the same old den, stayed here from the 16th of August to 12th September [1853]. On the 11th of September at 8 o'clock p.m., a message came to me that there had been a state room taken on the steamer City of Richmond for my benefit, and I assured the party that it would be occupied if God be willing.

Before 10 o'clock the next morning, on the 12th, a beautiful September day, I arose early, wrote my pass for Norfolk, left my old den with many a goodbye, turned out the back way to 7th Street, thence to Main, down Main behind 4 night watch to old Rockett's and after about 20 minutes of delay I succeeded in reaching the state room. My conductor was very much excited, but I felt as composed as I do at this moment, for I had started from my den that morning for liberty or for death providing myself with a brace of pistols."

"I didn't know I was a slave until I found out I couldn't do the things I wanted."

In the mid-1930s, fieldworkers of the **Federal Writers' Project** were assigned to travel through the Southern states to gather the life histories of ex-slaves. The ages of these former slaves now ranged from 75 to 100 and older. A set of simple instructions and questions helped get them to recall and talk freely about the time of slavery. Dozens of subjects were covered by the questions. The recollections and father-to-son traditions jotted down by the interviewers proved a folk history of slavery—"history from the bottom up"—that added evidence to such slave narratives as Northup's story, recorded during the abolitionist period.

"I didn't know I was a slave until I found out I couldn't do the things I wanted." That was how an old ex-slave put it when he was asked how it felt to be in bondage during childhood. *—ex-slave in Virginia*

WHY AM I A SLAVE?

Why are some people slaves, and others masters? Was there ever a time when this was not so? How did the relation commence?

These were the perplexing questions which began now to claim my thoughts, and to exercise the weak powers of my mind, for I was still but a child, and knew less than children of the same age in the free states. As my questions concerning these things were only put to children a little older, and little better informed than myself, I was not rapid in reaching a solid footing. By some means I learned from these inquiries, that "God, up in the sky," made everybody; and that he made white people to be masters and mistresses, and black people to be slaves.

This did not satisfy me, nor lessen my interest in the subject. I was told, too, that God was good, and that He knew what was best for me, and best for everybody. This was less satisfactory than the first statement; because it came, point blank, against all my notions of goodness. It was not good to let old master cut the flesh off Esther, and make her cry so. Besides, how did people know that God made black people to be slaves? Did they go up in the sky and learn it? or, did He come down and tell them so. All was dark here.

It was some relief to my hard notions of the goodness of God, that, although he made white men to be slaveholders, he did not make them to be bad slaveholders, and that, in due time, he would punish the bad slaveholders; that he would, when they died, send them to the bad place, where they would be "burnt up." Nevertheless, I could not reconcile the relations of slavery with my crude notions of goodness.

Then, too, I found that there were puzzling exceptions to this theory of slavery on both sides, and in the middle. I knew of blacks who were not slaves; I knew of whites who were not slaveholders; and I knew of persons who were nearly white, who were slaves. Color, therefore, was a very unsatisfactory basis for slavery.

Once, however, engaged in the inquiry, I was not very long in finding out the true solution of the matter. It was not color, but crime, not God, but man, that afforded the true explanation of the existence of slavery; nor was I long in finding out another important truth, viz: what man can make, man can unmake.

The appalling darkness faded away, and I was master of the subject. There were slaves here, direct from Guinea; and there were many who could say that their fathers and mothers were stolen from Africa—forced from their homes, and compelled to serve as slaves. This, to me, was knowledge; but it was a kind of knowledge which filled me with a burning hatred of slavery, increased my suffering, and left me without the means of breaking away from my bondage. Yet it was knowledge quite worth possessing.

I could not have been more than seven or eight years old, when I began to make this subject my study. It was with me in the woods and fields; along the shore of the river, and wherever my boyish wanderings led me; and although I was, at that time, quite ignorant of the existence of the free states, I distinctly remember being, even then, most strongly impressed with the idea of being a free man some day. This cheering assurance was an inborn dream of my human nature—a constant menace to slavery—and one which all the powers of slavery were unable to silence or extinguish.

—*from **The Narrative of the Life of Frederick Douglass, 1845***

What was slavery like as a way of living? By the 1830s, ex-slaves, freed or runaway, were beginning to tell their stories in print. Many of these tales were very widely read. Their fascinating details and dramatic adventures carried a powerful anti-slavery message. The narrative of **Josiah Henson** so impressed **Harriet Beecher Stowe** that when she wrote her novel *Uncle Tom's Cabin*, **Henson** was the model for her hero.

When the Civil War ended, 180,000 black troops had served in President Lincoln's army and 30,000 in the Navy. A quarter of a million had helped the military as laborers. To put an end to slavery, more than 38,000 blacks gave their lives in battle.

Black troops met their first major battle test in the storming of Fort Wagner. It was a Confederate stronghold on Morris Island, South Carolina, just six miles away from St. Helena Island, where Charlotte Forten was teaching the former slaves.

Placed at the head of the assault was the Massachusetts Fifty-fourth. Not a man of this first black regiment to be raised in the free states had held a musket in his hand eighteen weeks before. Without training in storming a fort, they were sent headlong into a badly planned night attack. The Confederate batteries answered with volcanic blasts of shots and shell, but the black soldiers climbed up the parapet to a desperate bayonet struggle at the top. Outnumbered and outgunned, they were ordered back after two assaults.

The Union casualties were great, and the Fifty-fourth bore the heaviest losses in dead and wounded. But the black troops had proved their courage and their soldiership.

Letters from the front gave the folks back home some idea of what the black troops were going through. One from **Lewis Douglass (son of Frederick Douglass)** told his sweetheart, **Amelia Loguen (daughter of J.W. Loguen)**, of the battle at Fort Wagner:

"WHEN FREEDOM COME, folks left home, out in the streets, crying, praying, singing, shouting, yelling, and knocking down everything. Some shot off big guns. Then come the calm. It was sad then. So many folks done dead, things tore up, and nowheres to go and nothing to eat, nothing to do. It got squally. Folks got sick, so hungry. Some folks starved nearly to death. Ma was a cripple woman. Pa couldn't find work for so long when he mustered out." —**Lewis Douglass**

NORTH CAROLINA

"AFTER US COLORED FOLKS was 'sidered free and turned loose, the Ku Klux broke out. Some colored people started to farming, like I told you, and gathered the old stock. If they got so they made good money and had a good farm, the Ku Klux would come and murder 'em. The government builded schoolhouses, and the Ku Klux went to work and burned 'em down. They'd go to the jails and take the colored men out and knock their brains out and break their necks and throw 'em in the river.

*There was a colored man they taken, his name was **Jim Freeman**. They taken him and destroyed his stuff and him 'cause he was making some money. Hung him on a tree in his front yard, right in front of his cabin.*

There was some colored young men went to the schools. Some white woman said someone had stole something of hers, so they put them young men in jail. The Ku Klux went to the jail and took 'em out and kill 'em.

After the Ku Kluxes got so strong, the colored men got together and made the complaint before the law. The governor told the law to give 'em the old guns in the commissary, what the Southern soldiers had used, so they issued the colored men old muskets and said protect themselves. They got together and organized the militia and had leaders like regular soldiers. They didn't meet 'cept when they heard the Ku Kluxes were coming to get some colored folks. Then they was ready for 'em. They'd hide in the cabins, and then's when they found out who a lot of them

Ku Kluxes was, 'cause a lot of 'em was kilt. They wore long sheets and covered the hosses with sheets so you couldn't recognize 'em. Men you thought was your friend was Ku Kluxes, and you'd deal with 'em in stores in the daytime, and at night they'd come out to your house and kill you.
                                        —from ***Lay My Burden Down***

When abolitionist Frances Kemble published her private journal in 1863, she caused quite a stir! The former English actress had moved to Philadelphia to get married. Her husband, Pierce Butler, later inherited a large slave plantation in Georgia. During an extended visit, Frances recorded detailed observations about how the slaves were treated. Her candid tales soon spread throughout America and England as more and more people read the truth.

LANGSTON HUGHES

Langston Hughes was born in 1902, in Joplin, Missouri. It was just at the time the Niagara Movement was crystallizing out of opposition to **Booker T. Washington's** policies. He grew up in Lawrence, Kansas, the town that had been a battlefield in **John Brown's** struggle to make Kansas a free state. His grandmother, who raised him till he was twelve, was the widow of **Sheridan Leary**, one of John Brown's men killed in the raid on Harpers Ferry. The boy's first job was to clean the lobby and toilets of an old hotel near his school, for which he got 50 cents a week. Then his grandmother died, and his mother took care of him, moving the family to Illinois and then to Ohio.

When he graduated from elementary school, his classmates elected him Class Poet, although he had never written a poem, because there was no one else around to fill the post, and blacks were all supposed to have rhythm. He had to produce something for the occasion, and that was how he started to write poetry. Later during the Harlem Renaissance (1920s-1940s), dozens of young writers flowered. Most of them wrote about black themes. The young **Langston Hughes**, who had moved to Harlem, became the unofficial poet laureate of his people and one of America's leading writers. He wrote poems, plays, short stories, novels, essays, history, biography, newspaper columns, and even lyrics for opera composers.

In his autobiography, Hughes tells what it was like in 1916 to be a high school boy and a Black American, in Cleveland, Ohio during World War I.

Just because I loves you —
That's de reason why
My soul is full of color
Like de wings of a butterfly.

Just because I loves you
That's de reason why
My heart's a fluttering aspen leaf
When you pass by.

The mills
That grind and grind,
That grind out steel
And grind away the lives
Of men —
In the sunset their stacks
Are great black silhouettes
Against the sky.
In the dawn
They belch red fire.
The mills —
Grinding new steel,
Old men.

Carl Sandburg's poems
Fall on the white pages of his books
Like blood-clots of song
From the wounds of humanity.
I know a lover of life sings
When Carl Sandburg sings.
I know a lover of all the living
Sings then.

LETTERS

TROY, ALA., OCT. 17, 1916

Dear Sirs: I am enclosing a clipping of a lynching again which speaks for itself. I do wish there could be sufficient pressure brought about to have federal investigation of such work. I wrote you a few days ago if you could furnish me with the addresses of some firms or co-opporations that needed common labor. So many of our people here are almost starving... quite a number here would go anywhere to better their conditions. If you can do anything write early as possible.

ANNISTON, ALA., APRIL 23, 1917

Dear Sir: Please gave me some infamation about coming north i can do any kind of work from a truck gardin to farming i would like to leave here and i cant make no money to leave i just make enough to live one please let me here from you at once i want to get where i can put my children in schol.

Dear Sir: I saw your add in the *Chicago Defender* for laborers. I am a young man and want to finish school. I want you to look out for me a job on the place working morning and evening. I would like to get a job in some private family so I could continue taking my piano lesson I can do anything around the house but drive and can even learn that. Send me the name of the best High School in Chicago. How is the Wendell Phillips College. I have finish the grammar school.

MOBILE, ALA., APRIL 25, 1917

Sir: I am a poor woman and have a husband and five children living and three dead one single and two twin girls six months old today and my husband can hardly make bread for them in Mobile. This is my native home but it is not fit to live in.

BIRMINGHAM, ALA., MAY 1917

Sir: i am in the darkness of the south and i am trying my best to get out do you no where about i can get a job in new york. i wood be so glad if cood get a good job... o please help me to get out of this low down county i am counted no more thin a dog help me please help me o how glad i wood be if some company would send me a ticket to come and work for them no joking i mean business i work if i can get a good job.

—from the *Journal of Negro History*, July and October, 1919

TENANT FARMERS

"I AIN'T GOT NO children and me and my husband works a one-horse farm and we got 'bout thirty acres. Last year we made six bales of cotton and rented the thirty acres for $60; fifteen acres we used for cotton, the rest for corn. We kept the corn and didn't sell none hardly. At ten cents a pound the six bales would bring $300. We had $10 advanced for four months. We turned it all over, and they took out the $40 advances, $30 for fertilizer, and $60 rent. We got through and then they say we come out $72.43 in the hole..."

"Last year I drawed $10 to the plow (meaning $10 a month for from four to six months for each 20 acres cultivated), but I ain't getting but $7 this year. I rents the whole place (400 acres) and then subrents it, and pays four bales of cotton for rent. But I don't never make nothing offen it. Didn't clear nothing last year. I paid out $200 last year. Interest steps on me time I pay me rent (for money borrowed from the bank) and interest cost 15 cents on the dollar. I haven't made nothing since 1927. I clears $210 then and ain't cleared nothing since. I got 21 cents for cotton that year. We farms 60 acres and pays $150 for rent. That's $75 to the plow. They 'vances us $15 a month for five months. I come out jest $175 in the hole."

"We run a two-horse farm. We was due to pay $150 rent last year, but I don't know what us is paying this year. We cut down on the land we was using. We made 22 bales of cotton last year, and it was selling at 8, 9, and 10 cents when we turned it in to the man. We didn't git nothing back."

"We got right 'round sixty acres and one-half of it is cotton. We working on halves. We got a two-horse farm. My daughter got one and

I got one. I farmed with "Mr. P" last year. We had thirty acres over there and made five bales of cotton and paid $100 for rent. We gits $2 a month in cash and $10 in rations. We came out $200 in the hole last year."

"I works a one-horse farm on halves. I get 'bout $12 a month in rations. Last year I worked for the Tallahassee Mill Company, and made $9.75 a week. My wife was working by the day for 50 cents a day."

Trouble comes, trouble goes.
I done had my share of woes.
Times get better by 'n' by,
But then my time will come to die.
–from **The Shadow of the Plantation**

"THERE WAS NINE of us kids in the family and we all had to work a lot. I flunked two grades in school because of the unjust system we had to live under. I stayed out of school a lot of days because I couldn't let my mother go to the cotton field and try to support all of us. I had to decide which was more important, getting an education or letting my mother suffer along. When my father stopped working I had to stay out of school more than ever before.

I picked cotton and pecans for two cents a pound. I went to the fields six in the morning and worked until seven in the afternoon. When it came time to weigh up, so to speak, my heart, body and bones would be aching, burning and trembling. I stood there and stared the white men right in their eyes while they cheated me, other members of my family, and the rest of the Negroes that were working. They had their weighing scales loaded with lead and the rod would always be pointing toward the sky. There were times when I wanted to speak but my fearful mother would always tell me to keep silent. The sun was awful hot and the days were long. It was like being baked in an oven. When I went to bed at night, I could see bolls of cotton staring me right in the face."

"... I would look at my sisters and my heart would say... dear sisters, I wish you could have and enjoy some of the finer things that life has to offer. I would look at my brothers and my heart would cry... oh brothers, if you only knew what it's like to live and enjoy life, instead of working like bees all the time to stay alive. Then I would look at my parents and my heart would utter... some day I'll build you a castle, and you will never have to bend your backs in another field. Last and least, I would think to myself. I wished I had enough money to help the poor, and to build a playing center and a new church for our community. All these wonderful thoughts made me forget about my sorrow troubles, but as I stop day-dreaming I would be the saddest guy in the whole world.

My hands are like a history book. They tell a countless number of sad, sad stories. Like a flowing river they seem to have no end. The cost of survival was high. Why I paid it I will never know.

I got expelled from the Lee County Training School for asking for some equipment for our school. All of the facilities that I asked was necessary for the proper kind of education a student needs. The officials of the city refused to let me register to vote. They also notified the surrounding schools not to let me enroll. I went to Shreveport, Lousiana, the 29th of September. I attended the Washington High School there for two weeks. I was really enjoying myself and I was learning an awful lot of things that I had never heard of before. The standards of the school is one of the higher that can be found in the U.S. I talked with the F.B.I.'s and shortly afterward white people started riding by the house. They started calling the lady that I was living with, hanging the phone up once she answered it. She told me that she didn't want her home bombed, and I had to leave."
—*Statement to Student Nonviolent Coordinating Committee,*
by **Charlie H. Wingfield, Jr.**, *Terrell County, Ga.*

U.S. CONSTITUTION
THE FIFTEENTH AMENDMENT
"The right of citizens of the United States to vote shall not be denied or abridged by the United States or by any State on account of race, color, or previous condition of servitude."

"... I've always believed that one day, even if I didn't live to see it, this country would be different. It would be a place for all people to live, where they could be without the hangings and the lynchings and the killings and the bombings. We are our brother's keeper whether he is black, white, brown, red or yellow. As the Bible tells us, God has made of one blood all nations."
—**Fannie Lou Hamer**